*Quick*GUIDES
everything you need to know...fast

Fundraising From Companies

by Jill Ritchie

reviewed by Sophie Moss

WIREMILL
PUBLISHING LTD

Across the world the organizations and institutions that fundraise to finance their work are referred to in many different ways. They are charities, non-profits or not-for-profit organizations, non-governmental organizations (NGOs), voluntary organizations, academic institutions, agencies, etc. For ease of reading, we have used the term Nonprofit Organization, Organization or NPO as an umbrella term throughout the *Quick*Guide series. We have also used the spellings and punctuation used by the author.

Published by
Wiremill Publishing Ltd.
Edenbridge, Kent TN8 5PS, UK
info@wiremillpublishing.com
www.wiremillpublishing.com
www.quickguidesonline.com

British Library Cataloguing in Publication Data
A catalogue record for this book is available from the British Library.

ISBN Number 1-905053-00-2

Printed by Rhythm Consolidated Berhad, Malaysia
Cover Design by Jennie de Lima and Edward Way
Design by Colin Woodman Design

Disclaimer of Liability
The author, reviewer and publisher shall have neither liability nor responsibility to any person or entity with respect to any loss or damage caused or alleged to be caused directly or indirectly by the information contained in this book. While the book is as accurate as possible, there may be errors, omissions or inaccuracies.

CONTENTS

FUNDRAISING FROM COMPANIES

INTRODUCTION

Companies support a range of nonprofit organisations (NPOs) through a range of methods. By such support, companies can achieve a number of objectives. They can associate their names and products with good causes. They can be good employers when supporting their employee's NPO activities. They can be good corporate "citizens," helping the communities where they work to prosper.

Many companies have clear criteria regarding the types of NPOs they support and specific ideas about the charitable pursuits – education, children, the elderly, health or the arts – that best fit their corporate purposes. The criteria regarding NPOs to be supported will depend on the analysis by the company of its business interests, geographical interests, employees' interests and broad social interests.

A company's charitable support might be organised by a structured social-investment office, the human resources department or the public relations office. The type of support given to NPOs will also vary among companies as will the extent of their involvement with the NPOs they support.

Reviewer's Comment
Sometimes a company does not have one person or department solely responsible for its charitable activity. It may be that the person who is responsible has a key job within the company and only works with NPOs as an extra responsibility. If this is the case, it is necessary to take into account that working with you may not be his or her top priority and things may move more slowly.

In sum, each company is different, and the way it looks at and acts upon its support for NPOs depends on the company, its products or services, and the way that it feels social responsibility will aid its commercial activities.

RESEARCHING CORPORATE INTERESTS

In order to appeal to companies for their support, one must first establish their giving criteria. This can be done in a number of ways:

- Visiting their Web sites
- Telephoning the company and asking
- Reading their annual reports
- Writing to the appropriate person in the company
- Talking to employees
- Talking to other organisations that receive funds from them
- Meeting the appropriate person

Reviewer's Comment

One fundraiser maintains that a great way to find companies that might support your activities is to go outside your premises and walk or bicycle around. Every company within a measurable distance should be considered as a potential supporter. This is particularly true for NPOs with a local remit and companies with a strong local presence.

Once you have found out that a company will consider supporting the type of activities entered into by your organisation, you should also establish how the company would like to be approached. This approach could be made in one of the following ways:

- Completing an application form provided by the company
- Writing a funding proposal within the company's guidelines
- Writing your own proposal

You will also need to establish what types of support you might request and the extent of that support. If, for example, you have a good case for gifts-in-kind support because you are an aid agency and your target is a pharmaceutical company, then you should focus your request on this possibility rather than a broad request for assistance.

Continued on Page 6

The important thing is that you find out what will benefit the company rather than what will most benefit the NPO. The company is not acting out of selfless disinterest – it is making decisions based on what will ultimately benefit it best. You stand a much better chance of obtaining funding if your homework on the company leads to an informed application or proposal highlighting the benefits to the company as well as the needs of the NPO.

Reviewer's Comment

Find out the proper person within the company with whom you should communicate. Find out whether the person is a male or female if it isn't obvious from the name. There is nothing worse than getting the gender wrong, misspelling the name or using the wrong job title.

Remember that it is not always necessary to approach large, national companies for support. As the saying goes, "Think global, act local." Don't neglect potential support, both in cash and in kind, from local small and medium-sized businesses. The corner store where an NPO's staff regularly makes purchases is a good potential source of support. A local bakery could be asked to deliver bread to a residential facility. A gardening service might undertake to maintain an organisation's gardens. Smaller local employers may be asked to allow a payroll-giving initiative or other type of support among their staffs.

Many companies adopt one or more "preferred NPO" partners. These NPOs not only receive donations, gifts-in-kind, staff expertise and other voluntary help, but they also are assisted on an ongoing basis through different fundraising events involving staff and/or customers of the company. The relationship between the company and NPO can be seen almost as a partnership for the benefit of both the partners.

To see if a company has a structured process for choosing an NPO partner, go through all of the methods discussed in the previous section in the context of identifying the company's charitable interests. However, even if a company has never considered an NPO partner, don't be afraid to ask if it would be open to the idea. A company may not have considered the possibility, and you could become its partner without the competition with other organisations that a structured selection process involves.

Reviewer's Comment

Partnerships may be called different things in different countries. Often they are called NPO of the Year partnerships. This does not mean that they will always last only a year. Increasingly, companies feel that building a successful relationship between a company and an NPO takes at least two years, if not longer.

The methods of company support listed in the following sections could be given by a company as part of an NPO partnership or preferential NPO relationship, or could be provided on a one-off basis. A company may support an NPO through one method or a number of methods. Obviously, it is best for an NPO to encourage a company to support it in as many ways as possible as well as to build up a long-term relationship that will benefit both organisations.

DONATIONS

A company may simply make a donation of money to your organisation and ask for nothing in return other than perhaps a thank you and acknowledgment of the donation. These donations are few and far between.

They may result from something as simple as asking the company for a donation (particularly with smaller companies where the owner is much in evidence) or they may happen when a company wants to be seen to be a supporter of your organisation in your literature or other materials.

A donation may also kick-start a relationship between the organisation and company that becomes long-term or encompasses staff or other funding methods.

As with all good fundraising practice, the donor company should be appropriately thanked for its donation no matter what size the donation is, not least because the company may be testing the NPO with the thought of larger donations and more involvement in the future.

Do not be afraid to ask the company how it wishes to be thanked. It may want to send an executive to one of your events, or it may want to be acknowledged in your literature in a particular way. It is the job of the NPO to ascertain how best to recognise the company's support, but input from the company could be very valuable.

A company may encourage its staff to support a particular NPO or to raise a designated sum or more for an NPO. The NPO may want to ask someone who works at the company to act as its representative among the staff member's colleagues, to encourage donations and fundraising activities.

The simplest way for staff to support an NPO is through personal donations, often through payroll giving as discussed later in this Guide. Donors should be treated as individuals and thanked as you would thank any donor as well as within the context of the company where they work.

Another way for staff to support an NPO is by engaging in fundraising activities on behalf of the NPO. It is then up to the NPO to work with the company to create ideas that will help staff raise this money. These ideas can incorporate a broad range of fundraising events including sporting activities like golf days, sponsored activities like giving up coffee for a period of time or shaving one's head, or going on overseas treks or other challenges.

Some ideas may be just for the company staff, while other ideas may have staff joining in with events already planned by the organisation.

The most successful fundraising events planned specifically for a company's staff are those that include as many people as possible, are quick and easy for staff to set up and run, or are memorable and great fun.

The most successful events already planned that staff members can join are those where they join with colleagues as an identifiable unit, such as in team sports activities or at a table at an event. Participants not only enjoy the event because they are with colleagues, but the company also receives publicity because it is being represented at the event.

With payroll-giving plans, a company's staff members allow a deduction from their wages or salary to be given to a specific NPO. This should be voluntary, and employees should not be pressured into participating. Payroll giving is an ideal way for workers to contribute small amounts to good causes and is often the manner in which many people make their first donations.

This sort of fundraising usually involves a representative of the NPO making a presentation to the company employees, explaining the way payroll-giving works. Many successful payroll-giving initiatives have staff giving only a small amount per week. If each member of the staff in a large company gives something regularly through a payroll-giving plan, it can add up to sizeable, regular and planned income for an NPO. It can also provide an entry through which individuals become involved with the NPO.

Payroll-giving relationships tend to last a long time. If such an initiative exists between a company and a certain NPO, it can often but not always be an exclusive relationship. It is good to maintain staff interest in your organisation by regularly publishing success or human-interest stories about the work you do in the company's staff newsletters, in your own newsletter or on the company's intranet. It is vital to nurture these company employee donors. They must be made to feel like partners – partners without whom the organisation could not do its work and its beneficiaries would be worse off. This may also encourage them to do more to support your NPO by organising fundraising events, becoming volunteers, leaving a bequest or recruiting other donors.

When new people join a company, they should be offered the opportunity to participate in the payroll-giving programme. This will increase the number of donors and replace those who drop out of the programme. You will need to talk to the company about ensuring that brochures or other information is available to new employees as well as current employees who may not already be participating.

Companies may already run or sponsor events – for staff, customers or for the general public – such as balls, Christmas parties, golf days or other sporting tournaments that could be used as fundraising events for your NPO. Money can be charged for entry to the event, and a company's suppliers can donate items for auction at the event.

Alternatively, an NPO can run its own event and sell a table to the company, enrol company teams or give places at the event to corporate supporters, or use company products as gifts for those attending the event. Companies may also provide sponsorship for an event – the venue, printing, organisation assistance or publicity. Although it may suit a company to participate in an NPO's event, this is more costly and more time-consuming for the NPO than giving a fundraising angle to an event that a company already runs.

An NPO can also organise treks or challenges for individuals from different companies or for individuals within a specific company. These could range from climbing Everest to trekking across the Sahara to bicycling across

Cuba. They may be related to the NPO's objectives (such as horse riding with wildlife in Africa, organised by a wildlife organisation) or just provide an interesting challenge to the participants. These treks or challenges rely on the participant obtaining sponsorship (funding) from friends, families and others that is then donated to the NPO. The NPO can support participants by providing fundraising ideas and online fundraising pages to help them raise as much money as possible as easily as possible.

Reviewer's Comment
There are companies that organise treks and challenges for groups of individuals who are interested in doing the trek or challenge and thus supporting the NPO. By talking to these companies and promoting their brochures and Web sites to your corporate supporters, you can offer your supporters a choice of challenges to undertake on your behalf at no cost to your organisation – individuals will raise sponsorship to cover their own costs and donations to you before they are allowed to take part in the challenge.

Companies can also support NPOs by allowing their staff members to volunteer their services and time free of charge and without counting the time off work as holiday.

Volunteering can take two forms.

Companies may provide volunteers with marketing, public relations, accounting, legal or other expertise. Such staff can work for an NPO on a regular basis such as one day a month or on an as-need basis. In some cases, companies might even send experts to an NPO for a number of months to work on a specific project.

When people are working at an NPO, ensure that you support them and their company by making sure other NPO staff members know why they are there and by providing information about the company that has given them time to volunteer.

Companies may also provide groups of employees to NPOs to complete tasks not necessarily aligned with their jobs (for example, painting and decorating part of a centre or facility). These kinds of projects are fantastic team-building experiences for the staff involved. And because they are done on company time, they do not impinge on the employees' free time.

Again, make sure that the company is identified. T-shirts with the name of the charity and the name of the company is just one way that recognition can be offered.

Reviewer's Comment
Some companies will even give a donation for every day their employees volunteer to help your organisation, as part of a matching-gifts programme.

Reviewer's Comment
You might want to consider appointing someone at the NPO to look after the volunteer, at least initially. The volunteer will take back to his or her company information about the experience encountered at the organisation.

MATCHING GIFTS

Some companies have programmes whereby they match donations and/or volunteer hours by their employees. Sometimes these matching gifts by the companies will be 1-to-1, and others may be as much as 3-to-1. Some companies extend their programmes to former staff or directors.

Some companies have specific rules regarding the type of organisations. Some will match gifts made to organisations in certain sectors like education, the arts or animals. Others will match gifts to any NPO regardless of the work it does.

It is important that you always ask supporters if the company they work for matches donations or volunteer activities, and ensure that you and your supporters take all required steps to obtain the matching gifts for which you qualify. It is important that you give all the required information to the company. This provides the company with a good impression of your organisation, which is always a good thing because you may at some time be asking that same company for support by other methods.

Many companies and employees see their matching-gift programmes as an incentive to attract and retain good staff. In some cases, matching gifts serve to introduce an NPO to a company and pave the way for the company itself to become interested in the NPO and its work.

NPOs can work with companies to raise money by producing merchandise that companies then sell to their staff members and customers in their office reception areas, stores or other outlets.

For example, a special teddy bear might be made available by a zoo for resale in a chain of children's stores with proceeds from the sales going to the zoo.

Reviewer's Comment

The most successful type of NPO merchandise is an inexpensive item that people want to purchase anyway but will be more likely to buy in order to support an NPO. Bookmarks and ties are examples. People will buy these items for themselves or for others as cheap, fun gifts.

Companies can also promote your events and other fundraising activities to their customers in order to encourage them to donate and/or take part.

By promoting your NPO to customers, the company is making a public statement that it supports your organisation and its work.

It is imperative that you treat the company's customers well. Nothing is worse than a company promoting an NPO and then getting complaints from customers about the event they went to or the response they received after making a donation. Failure to look after the company's customers can ruin a relationship with the company.

RECYCLING

Recycling plans are those whereby items are recycled and the recycling company pays an amount per recycled item to the NPO. Tin cans and stamps used to be the most common forms of recycling, but mobile phone, toner and printer-cartridge recycling have become increasingly popular and profitable for NPOs.

There are many companies that will work with you and your corporate partners to recycle these items. (To find a local company, search on the Internet under the type of recycling you would like to become involved in.) These recycling companies will supply envelopes or boxes to your corporate supporters to put in their offices, retail outlets, etc.

Staff and customers simply put their telephones or cartridges inside envelopes or boxes and send them to the recycling company free of charge. (Some recycling companies even offer a free collection service.)

Reviewer's Comment
The most successful recycling plans are those that are well promoted and that make it as easy as possible for people to recycle.

Companies can encourage recycling by including incentives for those who recycle their items; for example, each time a person recycles a certain number of cartridges, he or she receives a voucher to spend at the company's shop.

This also increases the company's sales because people will return to the store to redeem their vouchers and make other purchases.

Cause-related marketing is a commercial practice whereby a company and an NPO join together to market a product or service for mutual benefit. The company sells more products, and the NPO receives a fee for endorsing the products or services.

The NPO will endorse products that fit within its objectives, and the company will seek NPOs whose endorsement will make its products or services more attractive and saleable. For example, an NPO that promotes healthy living might link its name and logo to products such as low-cholesterol margarine or mineral water, while an organisation involved in cancer awareness might endorse sunblocks. For this kind of relationship to work, there should be a link or affinity between the NPO's cause and the product, brand or service that the company provides.

The endorsement of products by NPOs motivates people to buy the products or to engage the suppliers' services as the means of supporting a good cause, and this gives the company an edge over its competitors.

Depending on the product being endorsed, the endorsement often conjures up an impression of the product being superior to that of its competitors because an NPO is involved. Endorsements also have the bonus of promoting the NPO and its mission.

The public often perceives endorsement of a product or service to mean that the company automatically pays a percentage (usually quite nominal) to the NPO for every product sold. This is sometimes the case, but in many instances the NPO's logo is included on products for a prearranged annual fee.

Reviewer's Comment
Don't let false perceptions stand. If customers of a company believe that you receive a donation per sale, they may be unhappy if they learn it isn't true.

CAUSE-RELATED MARKETING

After estimating the number of particular products sold in a year, the donation that an NPO actually receives may be disappointing. In practice, it is a good idea to establish the relationship by agreeing on a minimum initial donation from the company to your NPO, which will be income that can only grow if more items than expected are sold.

It is imperative to have a binding agreement to protect both parties. The company is, in effect, leasing the logo of the NPO for a fee. The company may request exclusivity. For example, a pet-food manufacturer linking up with an animal-welfare organisation might insist that it be the only producer of pet food carrying the NPO's logo. The NPO can, however, still be involved in a campaign with another product such as flea powder or dog collars.

It is strongly advised that lawyers draw up a contract. The contract should, among other items, spell out time frames involved. Three years is a good period, long enough for the NPO to benefit both financially and from a greater awareness of its logo while the company receives credibility. After this time, both parties can review the situation. If the corporation wishes to continue the arrangement but is not willing to substantially increase its contribution, it may be time for the NPO to offer its marketable commodity – its logo (and reputation) – elsewhere.

Reviewer's Comment
NPOs should look closely and investigate all potential corporate partners. Look at their annual reports and their Web sites, and talk to other NPOs that might have been involved with them. Don't be so grateful that they are interested in you that you don't do your homework. The worst possible scenario is to become involved with a company that has bad press or develops bad press. Your reputation will suffer.

COMPETITIONS WITH AN NPO ELEMENT

NPOs can benefit from some company sales initiatives involving competitions. Competitions for prizes that are run by companies are marketing drives aimed at creating awareness of their products or services and, of course, increasing their sales.

Most competitions require that entrants send in proof of having purchased a certain product – often the entry form is contained on packaging materials.

Competitions are usually supported by advertising to encourage the sale of the product, which is required as part of the entry criteria. When an NPO is involved, it gives the company another angle through which it can promote the competition.

Organisations benefit when companies make a donation for each entry as a way of encouraging participation in the competition. The challenge is for the fundraiser to approach companies and introduce the idea of linking a competition to the NPO. Rarely will a fundraiser receive a call from a company or advertising agency offering such a partnership.

Reviewer's Comment
It is vital to make sure that you know the laws that govern competitions in your location if you are asked to become involved with one. Many times there are substantial legal issues involved.

The Internet has provided exciting new opportunities for corporate support of NPOs by enabling companies to include information about the NPOs they support on the companies' Web sites, thus increasing the profile of the NPOs. A company may also include solicitations for donations to an NPO on its Web site, provide a direct link to an NPO's Web site or provide contact details so that potential donors can contact the NPO in other ways. In addition, an NPO may be able to offer companies the opportunity to put their logos or banners on the NPO's site for a fee.

AUCTIONS ONLINE

Live auctions, auctions by mail and silent auctions at events have long been regular and reliable mechanisms for NPO fundraising. Therefore, it's a natural progression for companies to sponsor auctions on the Internet. The secret to a successful online auction is to use a variety of media (online, print, radio, TV, mail, etc.) to promote the online auction as much as possible and encourage people to seek it out. Few people are going to stumble upon an online NPO auction by accident. A company can become involved by donations of products for the auction, provision of space on the company's Web site with a link to the auction site, or assistance with IT and technical issues.

Reviewer's Comment
Commercial-auction Web sites sometimes give NPOs the opportunity to auction their items. No matter where your auction appears, it will only succeed with a high degree of publicity, a requirement that can be expensive and/or time-consuming to fulfil, particularly in relation to the amount that can reasonably be expected to be made from the auction.

FUNDING WITH A TAX BENEFIT

Many countries offer tax benefits to companies that support NPOs. For example, the company may pay less tax because it makes donations to NPOs. Or it may pay less tax because it has made donations of its products.

In some countries, companies are able to identify and pay certain expenses on behalf of NPOs from funds before they are subject to tax. This is beneficial to the company because it reduces its tax burden. Where this is permitted, it can be beneficial to the NPO because companies will then fund certain budgetary line items. These items could range from individual salaries to stationery to utilities.

Anyone who works for an NPO who is also going to be the person working with companies needs to familiarise himself or herself with the tax benefits available in his or her country or the country where the company is based. You don't need to become a tax expert, a lawyer or an accountant. But you do need to have a working knowledge of what is available.

Many staff members working for companies will themselves be very knowledgeable about the tax benefits available with respect to various types of donations. They may also be very knowledgeable about particular tax issues related to their own company. However, in other cases, staff members will know nothing, or very little, about their area, and any help you can give may, in turn, make giving to you a more attractive proposition.

Reviewer's Comment
In some countries, tax benefits will be a very important incentive to giving. In others, it may not be an issue at all. The more you can offer the company, the better chance you have of obtaining support.

GIFTS-IN-KIND

Many companies will donate the goods or services that they sell. These are usually known as gifts-in-kind. Gifts-in-kind can range from airline tickets given by an airline to stationery given by a printer to medical supplies given by a pharmaceutical company or courier services given by a courier firm. Or gifts-in-kind may be gifts of services such as free banking given by a bank, or free legal, accounting or administrative services given by firms that provide those services.

Companies can benefit from a gifts-in-kind arrangement because they don't need to use cash to support the NPO but can use products they already produce. Often the value of the product at the point of sale is much greater than the actual cost of production, so the donation is worth a lot but costs the company very little.

Potential donors are always impressed by the actions taken by an NPO to reduce expenses and will be impressed by gift-in-kind arrangements, which show sound management and good stewardship. The more products and services an NPO receives through gifts-in-kind, the smaller its cash fundraising target will need to be. So this type of arrangement can be very beneficial to both the company and the NPO.

It is important to give a monetary value to the gift in kind and to reflect this in some way in the financial accounting of your organisation. In some places, accounting regulations will require a particular manner of accounting for gifts-in-kind. Talk to your accountant and be sure you know the rules so that the NPO and company report the donation appropriately.

Sponsorship money is different from general NPO support in that it comes from a company's marketing budget. It is not a donation but a marketing opportunity for the company.

Companies spend money on anything from sponsoring the publication of a book or upgrading a community facility to mounting a cultural or sporting event – all with the full and sole intention of taking advantage of the accompanying brand awareness and advertising opportunities to sell more of their products or services and achieve greater brand recognition.

In addition, sponsorship is attractive to companies when it involves the interests of people who are part of the companies' target market groups (e.g., people who follow certain sports, cultural events, or issues related to domestic or wild animals).

Successful sponsorship deals are concluded when companies sponsor charitable events or activities that give them the opportunity to associate people from their target groups (i.e., their potential customers) with their brands through the sports, cultural events or charitable fields in which they are interested.

In the sponsorship relationship, the NPO can offer a company:

■ The opportunity to name the event after the company or include the company's name in the title of the event.

■ The opportunity for the company to advertise at the event or through related events.

■ Use of the company's logo in connection with the NPO's materials such as letterhead or newsletters.

The NPO receives money in exchange for sponsorship and can also benefit by increasing its profile through a highly publicised sponsorship arrangement.

Mutually beneficial sponsorship deals are concluded all of the time. You just need to look at the long-term sponsors of many sporting events as examples of successful sponsorship.

In order to encourage a company to sponsor an event or product, NPOs need to target companies to which the event has a specific and relevant link.

CONCLUSION

Company support for an NPO can include some or all of what has been covered in these pages. To gain and then nurture and maintain a company's support, you should make certain that you know a company's objectives in giving support and ensure that the NPO, when approaching the company, can show how these objectives are being achieved. Where possible, these objectives should be agreed on by the company and the NPO at the beginning of the partnership so that they are realistic. For example, some companies' main aims may be the attainment of PR through association with the NPO, while others may want to use their support to develop staff motivation and team building through organising and running fundraising events. If a company's objectives are achieved, it will be more enthusiastic about extending the period and extent of its work or partnership with your NPO, leaving everyone with good thoughts about the relationship.

JILL RITCHIE

Jill Ritchie started her own business at the age of 18 while also studying. By the time she was 28, she had created jobs for 120 people in a factory with seven retail outlets. At the same time, she was spending more time doing voluntary charity work than anything else. She then closed her business and entered the NPO sector as a member of the start-up team of the Triple Trust, the highly successful South African job-creation organisation, where she initially trained trainers and ran the organisation's marketing arm. After a year there, she took over the fundraising and, in five years, took the Triple Trust from a budget of South African Rand 100,000 per annum to Rand 9 million, most of which was raised from northern hemisphere donors. Jill left to start her own fundraising consultancy and book-publishing business, which she has run for the past 15 years. She has edited 3 books and written 15, 12 on fundraising, of which the best known is *Fundraising for the New Millennium.*

She has arranged numerous successful events for South African NPOs, raising both funds and friends for the organisations in the process. She has achieved much success in the field of cause-related marketing.

Jill is Vice President of the Southern Africa Institute of Fundraising and also heads up its Ethics Committee. She is in demand around the world as a speaker on fundraising.

Sophie Moss, Reviewer

Sophie Moss is part of the Company Fundraising Team at NCH, a large children's charity in the United Kingdom, and currently manages charity partnerships between NCH and a number of companies including Virgin Megastores and GM Daewoo. Her experience includes staff fundraising, organising fundraising events and winning and establishing "charity of the year" partnerships.

Prior to her fundraising experience, Sophie worked in marketing for five years.